the Little Book of Weed Games

Previously published as
Mr. Bud's Pot-Smoking Games

25 Hilarious Pot-Smoking Games
and Cannabis-Themed Activities to Spark Up Your Next Smoke Sesh!

 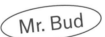 Mr. Bud   ILLUSTRATED BY Amanda Lanzone

ULYSSES PRESS

Published by:
Ulysses Press
PO Box 3440
Berkeley, CA 94703
www.ulyssespress.com

ISBN: 978-1-64604-628-7
Library of Congress Control Number: 2023947759

Printed in the United States
10 9 8 7 6 5 4 3 2 1

Project editor: Shelona Belfon
Proofreader: Yi-Yi Huang
Front cover design: David Hastings
Interior design: Jake Flaherty
Production: Winnie Liu
Artwork: © Amanda Lanzone except as noted on page 110

Contents

A Note from Mr. Bud

If you're like most stoners, you've got a crew of regulars you love to sit around and smoke with. You've probably got some rituals about where people sit, what you use to smoke from, what you watch once you're high—stuff like that. But as wonderful as all that is in its pure form, after a while a cipher can go a little stale. You've watched and rewatched every single episode of *Family Guy* and *South Park*. You've taken the same trek to 7-Eleven for a Slurpee of your own design (a mix of all the flavors, but mostly the blue one) enough times to rot your teeth out, and if someone brings up Phish again, you're going to freak out.

Well, Mr. Bud is here to save the day (or night)! With these 25 weed-errific games, you'll put the pizzazz back in your pot, the blast back in your bong, and the kink back in your kind bud. You'll throw dice, play cards, revive some dusty board games, and breathe smoke back into classic movies. I've even provided stoner versions for a few of your favorite childhood board games online at www.ulyssespress.com/books/the-little-book-of-weed-games. You'll never think about Candy Land the same way again.

Unlike in drinking games where you have to drink when you lose, the games in this book reward you with smoking. If you do well and win, you smoke—as it should be. There are a couple of games where I give the option to do the opposite, and smoke as a penalty, and really any game can be flip-flopped and played this way. But that makes no sense to Mr. Bud.

I recommend using dirt weed or even spliffs (if you're into the whole tobacco thing) to play the games in this book. If you use the fancy hydroponics shit, you're going to burn a lot of dough, cuz that stuff ain't cheap, and you're about to smoke a lot. And since you're going to smoke a lot, try to know your limits. Being super high is super fun! Being too high is just a paranoid bummer. So call it quits whenever you feel like you've had enough, or you could smoke yourself blind (Mr. Bud did that once—true story!).

OK, you've been warned! Now get going!

Dice and Deck Games

Turn boring old cards and dice into exciting new ways to get waaaaaay too friggin' stoned!

ZONK

One of the oldest weed games known to man, this game harkens back to ye olde 1970s. The ancient texts have been rewritten and revised countless times by forgetful stoners, so though no verifiably official rule set can be trusted absolutely, the version below is Mr. Bud's favorite. It may seem complicated at first, but trust me, the rules make a lot of sense once you get them down.

Object of the game

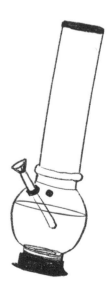

- ☙ Roll dice for points.
- ☙ Points get you bong hits.
- ☙ Bong hits make you happy.
- ☙ Highest score/player wins—really though, everyone who plays wins.

What you will need

- 5 dice

- 1 notebook

- 1 pen, pencil, or crayon

- 3 or more players

- Snacks never hurt

- 1 sucker to be the scorekeeper (they also get to be a player, so they should be somewhat trustworthy and be able to do simple addition under the influence—or at least own a calculator)

How to play

1. The youngest player rolls first to start the game. Gameplay goes clockwise. Each turn starts by rolling all 5 dice.

2. You must get at least one scoring die (see below for the down-low on scoring dice), or you zonk out and get 0 points. If at least 1 die scores you points, you can take those points and end your turn (if you're a total wuss, anyway).

3. Or you can gamble by rerolling the non-scoring dice to increase your score. You can stop after any successful gambling roll and take your

points and be all pleased with yourself. The only time you have to reroll is if you are using all 5 scoring dice.

Gambling rolls

1. You can reroll as many dice as you want, as long as at least 1 scoring die remains. For example, if you roll 2 scoring dice and 3 duds (like 2 fives, a two, a four, and a six), then you can reroll 4 of them (including one of the fives) as long as you keep 1 scoring die (the other five).

2. A die that is only a scoring die as part of a set cannot be rerolled. For example, say as part of your roll, you rolled 3 threes (and a couple of duds like a four and a six); you can't just keep 1 three and reroll the other 2. But you could reroll all 3 threes (as long as you keep at least one scoring die, duh). So you can:

But you are not allowed to:

Keep: 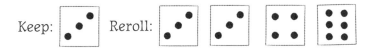 Reroll:

If you take this gamble and none of the dice you reroll scores points, then (wah wah!) you zonk out and lose all your points from that turn.

3. You can keep rerolling dice as long as you're hot and the dice keep scoring! Or you can stop after any scoring roll.

But: If you keep a die as a scoring die in one turn, that die cannot be rerolled in a subsequent turn. For example, say you keep a five as a scoring die and reroll the other 4 dice and get 3 threes and a two. You can keep the 3 threes as scoring dice and reroll the two to keep the hotness going, but you cannot also roll that five that scored for you on your first roll. You can only reroll the two.

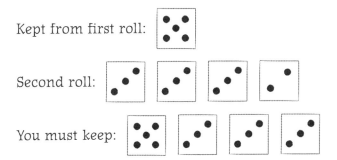

Kept from first roll:

Second roll:

You must keep:

You can keep those points or gamble and reroll the , but that's it.

4. If all five dice are scoring dice you want to keep, you must pick them up and roll them all again. Any additional points are added to your turn's score. If you get no scoring dice, you lose it all.

Score!

Here's how to get your points:

 is worth 50 points. is worth 100 points.

A Straight: These are worth 150 points. They must be 5 consecutive numbers one through five or two through six.

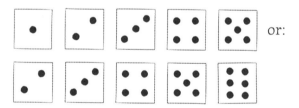 or:

Three of a Kind: Rolling 3 of the same number is worth 100 times the number. For example, 3 fives are worth 500 points:

 × 100 = 500 points.

This is true for all numbers except one—3 ones are worth 1,000 points.

 = 1,000 points.

Four of a Kind: Worth 100 times the number plus 500. For example, if you roll 5 fives, you get 100 × 5 + 500 = 1000!

 × 100 + 500 = 1,000 points.

Five of a Kind: Worth 100 times the number plus 1,000. For example, if you roll 5 fives, you get 100 × 5 + 1,000 = 1,500!

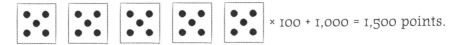 × 100 + 1,000 = 1,500 points.

Adding on to your score

Say you roll a one-three-six-four-four, you keep the one and roll the remaining 4 dice. If you roll two-three-four-five, then you have a Straight, i.e., even though the one was used as a scoring die of 100 points from your initial roll, it can be counted toward a Straight on a subsequent roll. You do not retain that 100 points from your first roll though. You just get the 150 points from the Straight, you greedy bastard.

First roll: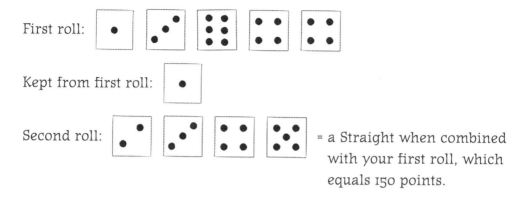

Kept from first roll:

Second roll: = a Straight when combined with your first roll, which equals 150 points.

Same goes if your second roll was a one-one-four-three. You can use the 2 newly rolled ones with your one from your first roll to get the 1,000-point 3-ones bonus.

First roll: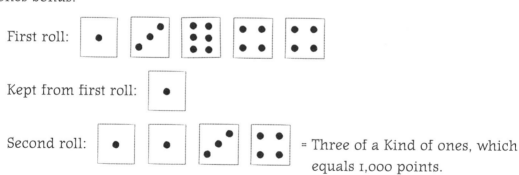

Kept from first roll:

Second roll: = Three of a Kind of ones, which equals 1,000 points.

How do I keep track of this shit!?

Keeping score is easy. Just write everyone's names, initials, or nicknames (less incriminating) across the top of a piece of lined paper, and draw vertical lines down the page to give each person a column. At the end of each person's turn, write down what happened. This will be:

🌫 Their points.

🌫 "Zonk" if they zonked (or whatever special roll happened—see below).

🌫 Add a star if they got a bong hit.

🌫 Draw a party if it was a social smoke.

    Have fun with it. You can record the start and end time, so you can marvel at how much you smoked in such a short time. If something hilarious happens along the way, leave a note so when you look back fondly on the score sheet, you still won't be able to remember what happened, but at least you'll know it was definitely awesome!

A	S	L
ZONK	300	200
650	650	700
1200☆	1000☆	1000☆
ZONK	ZONK	1300
2630☆	ZONK	ZONK
ZONK	1800	ZONK
3850	2300☆	3200
4:20	ZONK	3500
ZONK	ZONK	ZONK
5200☆	SPAZ	4:20☆
6400	2000	4600
7000☆	ZONK	ZONK
ZONK	4000☆	4000
E	4:20	5400
	N	6000☆
		D

So when do I smoke!?

1. Every time you get 1,000 points, you smoke.

2. Every time someone gets 4,200 points as the score at the end of their turn, it's a social and everyone smokes. Woot!

3. Every time someone breaks 10,000 points, it's a social and everyone smokes. Hooray!

So when do we stop!?

Whenever you want! You can set a points goal, play till you run out of weed, or roll on and on until you just can't roll anymore.

Special names, rolls, and rules

All sorts of weirdo things can and will happen as you play. Some of my favorites are below. You can incorporate them into your game or come up with your own house rules.

Klutz: If you are rerolling all 5 dice because you scored with all of them in one or multiple rolls, and on that 5-dice reroll you get no scoring dice, then you lose all your points on that turn and you're a klutz. Ugh, it's the worst!

Sloppy dice: If you roll 1 or more dice off the table or whatever surface you are playing on, you lose your points and your turn.

Whale's tail: If a die lands on top of 1 or more other dice, it's a whale's tail and you get a bonus 100 points on top of any other scoring die. If there are no other scoring dice, i.e, you zonked out, you get the 100 points, but your turn is over. If a whale's tail is suspected to be on purpose, all players (excluding the player whose turn it is) will vote on whether it was by accident or on purpose. If it is decided it was on purpose, you are a cheater and not only do you lose this turn but your next turn is also skipped. Shame!

Geeking it: If you drop the dice by accident while shaking them, you geeked it and you lose your turn, geek.

Double goodness: If you have 2 dice left and you risk rolling them and they come up as a (non-scoring) pair, you don't get any additional points, but you keep your points and reroll all 5 dice. But if you choke on the 5-dice reroll, as always, you lose all the points from that turn.

Lowest totem: Whoever has the lowest score has to do the bidding of the player with the highest score, getting chips, packing bowls, doing dances, all of it.

Nicknames: In the beginning of the game, everyone picks a nickname. If during the course of the game anyone accidentally calls someone by their real name instead of their nickname, that person loses their current turn if they're in the middle of rolling or their next turn.

CEE-HI

Why would you want to be low when you can get high? I have no idea either. That's why I play this game instead of the classic Cee-Lo.

Object of the game

🌿 Bet weed.

🌿 Win weed with the best roll.

🌿 Smoke weed.

What you will need

🌿 3 dice

🌿 3 players who all have weed

How to play

Everyone bets a certain amount of weed or hits. The youngest player rolls first. Gameplay goes clockwise. Roll all 3 dice until you get a scoring roll. If there's a tie at the end of the round, the tied players reroll until someone wins.

Score!

Scoring rolls ranked from awesomest to sorriest are:

If you roll this, you automatically win! Hooray! Unless someone gets the same roll—then it's tie-breaker time.

Tripping: If you roll 3 of a kind, you are trippin', son! The higher the trip, the better, duh. So 3 sixes beats 3 twos.

Pairing: If you roll a pair, then you're left with a leftover, and it's the leftover that counts as the score. So if you roll 2 sixes and a one, but someone else rolls 2 ones and a six, you're beat!

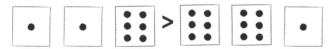

If you roll this combo, then everyone smokes all the weed bet at the beginning of the round. Let's hear it for communism!

 Remember how if you roll four-five-six, you automatically win? Well if you roll one-two-three then you automatically lose. Wah wah. It counts as a scoring roll, so you have to keep it, but it's the worst thing you can get that counts. The only thing that will save you is if everyone playing is the worst.

Anything else: is worthless and you have to reroll all the dice.

So when do I smoke!?

1. Whoever has the best roll wins the weed or hits bet at the beginning of the round.

2. If someone rolls four-two-one, then everyone smokes. Eff yeah, Cee-Hi!

TEXAS SMOKE 'EM

Well pardner, if you're anything like me, you've been lulled into a stoned, 18-hour trance of televised poker. There's something strangely compelling about it. Or maybe you've spent your own long night playing poker while getting lit. But you know what would be better than either of these? A poker game in which instead of playing for green, you played for the other green. Yee-haw!

Object of the game

🍃 Win hands.

🍃 Take hits.

What you will need

≋ A deck of cards (or more so you can alternate shuffling/dealing each deck)

≋ Chips (the poker kind, not the potato kind; well, also the potato kind) or coins that represent denominations of 5, 10, and 25

≋ 3 or more players, each with their own stash of weed

Pregaming information

The stakes are high!

Divvy up your chips or coins so everyone has an even pile. You want a bunch of 5s, half as many 10s, and only a few 25s. Each player puts an equal amount of weed into a communal pile.

Special cards

In Texas Smoke 'Em, red fours and black twos are always wild.

Who's what now?

The youngest person is the first "Dealer." They start so young these days . . . To indicate which person is the Dealer, place a token—like a button or a light bulb or some shit—in front of them. The job of Dealer rotates to the left after each hand, and that token gets passed along with the job.

The person to the Dealer's left is the "Lighter" and has to put in the obligatory "small blinds" bet, which is half that of the big blinds.

The person to the Lighter's left is the "Big Bong" and has to make an obligatory "big blinds" bet using the chips or coins. This is the minimum bet that any player can make for that hand. In addition to chipping in the big blinds, the Big Bong has to also pack the bowl for the winner of the hand.

Blinds leading the blinds

The blinds can go up throughout the game. This can happen each time the job of Dealer makes it back to the first person who had it, or it can go up when you get bored with everyone betting like pussies. Whenevs.

When the game gets down to 2 players, the blinds turn into an ante that is the equivalent of the minimum bet, and both players must pay it. Whoever isn't the Dealer is the one putting in the weed for that hand.

How to play

Note: If you already know how to play Texas Hold 'Em, then just do that and skip ahead to "So when do I get to smoke!?" to find out how to integrate your favorite pastime with your other favorite pastime. Remember though that red fours and black twos are wild in Texas Smoke 'Em!

Dealing and pre-flop

1. Starting with the person on their left, the Dealer gives each player 1 card until all the players have 2 cards. These are your pocket cards.

2. Now it's pre-flop bettin' time. The person to the left of the Big Bong can either match the big blinds/minimum bet, make a bet even bigger than that, or fold like some kind of pansy.

3. Betting goes around like that until it gets back to the Lighter. This person now has to put in however much money is needed to match the bet, or they can raise at this point, or they can fold and lose their small blind like an asshole. The amount they need to put in to match the bet includes the small blinds they put in, so if the small blinds were 25 and the bet is up to 50, they only need to put in 25 more.

4. The Big Bong now has to match the bet if the bet has been raised since they put in the big blinds, or they can fold like a jerk, or they can raise and keep the pre-flop flopping, or if no raise has been made to the bet, the Big Bong can check it by saying, "Check it!" and/or knocking on the table like the cool guys on TV.

Get floppy

5. Once everyone is in for the full bet, it's time to for the "flop." The Dealer burns a card by putting it face down so no one can see it, then laying down 3 cards face up—this is known as the flop. These cards are common

cards that everyone uses to try to make a good hand with their pocket cards.

6. Another round of betting ensues, starting with the Lighter, or the first person to the Dealer's left who is still in. This person can check it, bet, or fold if they're spineless.

Everything turns

7. Now it's time for the "turn." The dealer burns a card and lays a single card face up. This is another common card. Another round of betting, checking, and/or folding ensues, starting with the Lighter, or the first person to the Dealer's left who is still in.

Take it to the river!

8. The dealer burns a card and lays a final single card face up. This is another common card called the "river." A final round of betting, checking, and/or folding ensues, starting with the Lighter, or the first person to the Dealer's left who is still in, to determine the supreme lord of the hand.

Win!

To win a hand

You must be the only loser who didn't fold. In this case you don't have to show any of those losers your cards, because they're losers.

Or you face off in a bloody showdown of high-intensity action! Which basically means the remaining players complete the final round of betting. Then you lay your cards down to see who can make the best 5-card hand using their pocket cards and/or the common cards. You can use 1, both, or neither of your pocket cards and 3 to 5 of the common cards to make the best hand possible. Best cards win the hand, or if there is a tie, both tied players win. Yay!

Whoever made the last bet has to show their cards first (not the player who matched the bet, but the player who made/raised the bet). If the next person to the left of that better is beat, they do not need to show their cards—they can just say, "Fuck you! You beat me!" and sulk. But if they claim to have the better hand they have to show it.

To win the whole game

You must knock out all the other players and have all their chips.

Or if the weed runs out, whoever has the most chips gets the glory of being crowned supreme winner.

So when do I smoke!?

1. When you win the hand, of course! If there's a tie, all the winners smoke. The Big Bong must pack the bowl for you and the Lighter must light it.

2. At the end of the game, if there is still weed left in the communal pot and the winner won by getting everyone else's chips, the winner gets all the weed that's left. Score! The winner can smoke it all straight to their head or hoard it like some kind of stoner miser or throw it in the air and let it rain down on them or whatever the hell they want. It's their friggin' weed!

3. Or if the winner only won because they had the most chips when the weed ran out, then the person with the least chips (or the one who got knocked out of the game first) is in charge of getting the winner whatever munchies the winner wants.

Special hands

If a four and a two appear anywhere in any order in the common cards, it's a social and *everyone* smokes.

If a player gets a four and a two as pocket cards and stays in for the whole hand, they get a hit at the end of the hand. If they also win the hand, then they get two hits—one for winning and one for being a winner.

NOTE: Wild cards—red fours and black twos—can stand in for any other card of any suit. So you could use a two of spades to make a Royal Flush of hearts.

All suits are ranked equally.

If multiple players have the same type of hand—for example, two of you have a pair—the one with the highest pair wins, duh. So if you have a pair of fives and the other player has a pair of jacks, you're beat! But what if you both have a pair of jacks? Then whoever has the highest cards wins. So if you have 2 jacks, a five, a six, and a king, and your opponent has 2 jacks, a three, a seven, and a queen, you win!

ROYAL FLUSH: Your ass actually got 10, jack, queen, king, ace in the same suit. I hope you bet big! If in some weird *Twilight Zone* universe, multiple players lay down an RF, it's a tie (all suits are ranked equally).

STRAIGHT FLUSH: You got 5 consecutive cards in one suit, such as five, six, seven, eight, and nine of clubs.

FOUR OF A KIND: I don't have to tell you what this means, right?

FULL HOUSE: Well, Danny Tanner, you need a pair and 2 of a kind to make a Full House. If multiple players have this, the highest 3 of a kind wins, or if it comes down to it, the highest pair. Same hand? Splitskies!

FLUSH: Is it hot in here? Must be, cuz you just got 5 cards of the same suit! More than one flush? You guys are blowing that shit up! The Flush with the highest card wins.

STRAIGHT: If you've got 5 consecutive cards in a mix of suits, you're straight.

THREE OF A KIND: I'll give you one guess.

TWO PAIR: If you don't know this, don't play.

ONE PAIR: See Two Pair explanation.

HIGH CARD: It's a sad hand when whoever has the single highest card wins.

GUMMY

I bet when you learned to play Rummy on your granddad's knee, you never imagined that one day you'd be playing a tweaked-out version that gets you blazed. Well, my friend, that day has come! Get out your deck of cards and see if Gramps is interested in some holistic treatment for his glaucoma.

Object of the game

🌿 Get rid of all your cards.

🌿 Be the first to earn 420 points.

🌿 Smoke a bunch of weed.

What you will need

- A deck of cards
- 2 to 6 players
- A piece of paper to keep score on

How to play

What's the deal?

1. The youngest person deals first. Starting with the player to their left, they give 1 card at a time to each player until everyone has 6 cards unless there are only 2 players, then each player gets 10 cards.

2. After everyone has their cards, one card is dealt face up to start the "Trash Heap" and the rest of the stack is left as the "Stash Pile." The player to the left of the dealer goes first.

Picking up

1. You start a turn by taking from either the Trash Heap or the top face-down card on the Stash Pile. You can pick up as many cards as you want from the Trash Heap as long as you:

2. Use the very bottom card you pick up to throw down some scoring shit on that turn.

3. Don't discard the top card.

Throwing down

There are three different ways you can try to ditch the cards in your hand:

1. **Discarding:** When you discard, you lay the card face up next to the previous card in the Trash Heap. This way all the trashed cards will be visible. You must have a card to discard to end your hand, and that card cannot be the top card from the Trash Heap if you were a garbage picker on that turn.

2. **Melting:** You've got some scoring cards, such as Three of a Kind, Four of a Kind, or a "Piece of Straight," which is 3 sequential cards of the same suit. Throw that shit down in front of you!

   Note: Aces are as low as they go in this game, so a Piece of Straight can start with an ace and proceed to a two or it can end with a king, but it can't go queen, king, ace.

3. **Leeching:** If someone has thrown down a melt and you've got a card that can leech off their success, lay that sucker out. For instance, someone put down 3 threes and you've got the other three—that's a leech. Some other player put down four, five, six of spades, and you've got the seven of spades? Leech, baby!

I'm out!

A player goes out when they have no cards left, duh. This happens after a melt or leech is laid down, leaving the player with just one card in their hand, which they throw down on the discard pile and yell, "I'm out!"

Score!

Once some lucky bastard goes out, everyone adds up their score. Each player gets the points for the scoring cards they laid down, but the player who went out gets the points from all the cards left in all the other players' hands.

1. Face cards, i.e., kings, queens, and jacks, are worth 10 points each.

2. Aces are worth 1 measly point.

3. Number cards are worth their number, so a five is worth 5 points, and...do I really need to explain this any more?

4. Fours and twos double the points for the melt they're in. So if you laid down 3 fours, that's 12 points for the melt and then you double that and get 24 points. Rock! If you threw down a two to leech onto someone else's melt, you just get the value of the leech doubled, which is 4 points in this example.

5. Once you know your score, the scorekeeper jots it down.

SHOTGUNS, THE AWESOME KIND

When you shotgun smoke you are basically are blowing smoke into another person's mouth. You can do this a few ways:

1. The Easy Way

You take a hit, make tunnel with your hand, and blow the smoke through your hand tunnel into another person's mouth. If you like this person, and I mean like-like, you can blow it straight from mouth to mouth with no hand tunnel.

2. The Exciting Way

This is not for the faint of heart or the clumsy. When a blunt, joint, or spliff is burned about halfway to three-quarters of the way down, you take a small hit off it, turn it around, and place the lit end (the burning hot cherry) into your mouth. Don't burn your tongue. Obviously. Now hold the blunt/joint/spliff in place with your lips, basically the same way you'd hold it in your lips even if the burning ember wasn't now literally inside your head.

Another person now stands in front of you with their mouth open, real close, to the unlit end of the blunt/joint/spliff that's sticking out of your mouth. You blow, and the smoke will shotgun out like crazy into the other person's mouth. Everyone coughs and gets off. You can use the hand tunnel thing from "The Easy Way" if you want, but it's not necessary.

3. The Bong Way

If the bong you're using has a slide bowl that can be pulled fully out of the bong, then you can do things "The Bong Way." Person A fills the chamber of the bong up with smoke the regular way one smokes a bong. Get that shit nice and milky. Then person B comes along and puts their mouth where one normally does on a bong. Now person A removes the slide bowl from the bong and blows into the bong, forcing all the smoke in the chamber into person B's lungs. Person A can even include the hit they got when they were filling the chamber if they have the lung capacity for it.

Did I win!?

If you have the most points for a hand, you win the hand! But you only win the game if you are the first player to score 420 points.

So when do I smoke!?

Excellent question! There are two ways you smoke through this game:

Version #1 Gung-Ho Gummy

1. Every time you melt, you take a hit. Every time you leech, the person you are leeching off gives you a shotgun.

2. Whoever wins the hand gets a hit for every 50 points they scored. So if you earned 125 points, you get two hits.

3. Whoever wins the game wins a whole bowl-pack, bong-load, or spliff to their head. You can share if you're magnanimous. Or you can mock the losers. Either way.

Version #2 Gummy Regs

1. Whoever wins the hand gets a hit.

2. Whoever wins the game wins a whole bowl-pack, bong-load, or spliff to their head.

PEACE

So it's just you and your buddy hanging around, shuffling your feet, totally bored, wishing you had more friends who were down for a game of Zonk or something, but you don't. Well, that's no problem! You can bust out a deck of cards and play this game, which is sort of like the card game War, but better since you'll be getting high. In the tradition of hippies protesting wars with flower power, I've dubbed this game Peace.

Object of the game

🌿 Bring about peace by taking all your opponent's stuff.

🌿 Get wicked high!

What you will need

🌿 A deck of cards

🌿 2 players

How to play

Maintaining peace is harder than making war, so there's a little added strategy to this game.

Big deal

1. Deal the cards 1 at a time until each player has half the deck, i.e., 26 cards. Gather your 26 cards into a Peacetime Stockpile. Pick up the top 3 cards and hold them.

2. At the same time, you and your peacetime soulmate negotiate Peace by laying down 1 card from the 3 in your hand. Choosing which card is where the strategy comes in. And since there is this bit of stratagem in negotiating the Peace, it's crucial that you throw down at the same time, lest one of you be a pathetic cheater.

3. The highest card wins both cards, and they go to the bottom of your Peacetime Stockpile. After every round, you take another card off the top of your Peacetime Stockpile so that each player has 3 cards in their hands to start each round (until someone is losing big time and has fewer than 3 cards—so sad).

Peacetime!

4. If you both throw
down the same card,
as in you both throw
down a queen, then
it's Peacetime! From

your Peacetime Stockpile (not the 3 cards in your hand), you each lay 3
cards face down as the peace fuse, then light off the peace bomb by laying
the 4th card face up. Highest card obliterates their opponent into Peaces
and takes all the cards from the Peacetime. In the unlikely but-it-does-
happen event that the peace bombs (4th cards) are of equal flower-power
magnitude, you just Peacetime again and again until someone dominates.

Peace cards

5. Aces are hiiiigh in this game. Fours and twos are Diplomat cards,
meaning you throw one of those suckers down to prove your super
diplomacy skills and automatically win that round. They even beat aces.
But if you both throw down a Diplomat, you'll have one hell of a high-
stakes Peacetime on your hands.

Winning the Peace

The winner is whoever gets allllll the cards.

So when do I smoke!?

When you smoke depends on how dedicated to Peace you are. There are two levels:

Level #1 Pretty Keen on Peace

1. Every time a Diplomat card is played, the winner of the round tokes.

2. Every time a Peacetime comes around, the winner of the Peacetime takes a hit.

3. Whoever wins the game gets to kill the bowl, bong, joint, or whatever else was being smoked throughout the game.

Level #2 Peacemonger

1. Every time you win a round, you take a hit.

2. Every time a Diplomat card is played, the winner of the round tokes twice.

3. Every time a Peacetime comes around, the winner of the Peacetime takes 2 hits.

4. Whoever wins the game gets a fresh bowl-pack, bong-load, joint, or whatever was being smoked throughout the game. They can peacefully smoke it to the head, or generously share it to keep the Peace.

BONGHOLE

This game is a variation on the Japanese game Dai Hin Min. There are tons of variations out there, including the infamous drinking game Asshole. Bonghole is similar but better for a bunch of reasons, chief among them are that it involves weed instead of cheap beer and that at the end of the night you're much more likely to nap in a crumb pile of your own Doritos instead of pass out in a puddle of your own puke. Instead of making people drink as a punishment, you get to smoke as a reward. Life is better here.

Object of the game

≳ Get rid of all your cards first.

≳ Become the Bongmaster, not the Bonghole.

What you will need

- A deck of cards
- At least 4 players

Who's who

Bongmaster: The winner of the previous hand. The gloater, the boaster, the demander of snacks. This title bestows upon its owner the ability to command the Bonghole to do their bidding when it comes to procuring munchies, packing the bowl or rolling the joints, answering the doorbell, whatever.

Lightermaster: Second placer of the previous hand. The toady, the status climber, the guy holding the lighter. The only thing this person has to do is light the bowl, bong, or whatever that's being smoked.

Midi: The player who didn't out and out lose the last hand. The middle ground, the nobody, the who cares. This person is of no special note.

Bonghole: The last hand's big stinking loser. The wretched, the meek, the really pissed off. This player must do the Bongmaster's bidding and only spit in their drink if no one catches them.

How to play

Here's the deal

1. The youngest person deals the first hand. Starting with the player on their left and moving around the table, the dealer doles out all the cards one at a time. Each player needs to have the same number of cards, which is all well and good, but if you have 3, 5, or 6 players, you'll need to add some jokers or twos from another deck. Games with 3 or 6 players need to add 2 cards to the deck. Games with 5 players need to add 3 cards to the deck.

Ditching your cards

2. The player to the left of the dealer puts down a "Trick," which is a funny way of saying "cards of the same rank," which is an all-encompassing but somewhat vague way of saying "a single card, a pair, 3 of a kind, 4 of a kind (or 5 of a kind if you've got wild cards/jokers)."

3. The next player to the left has to then match that Trick or throw down the same Trick of a higher value. So if a pair of fours are on the table, the next player has to throw down a pair of fours or higher, such as a pair of fives.

4. Play travels around the table until no one can go or someone throws down a two, which is the supreme overlord of this game. Whoever was the

first to throw down all of their cards starts the next round by laying down whatever they damn well please.

Becoming the Bongmaster

To become the Bongmaster, you must be the first person to get rid of all your cards.

First hand

Everyone is on an equal footing, and there are no rank losers or regal winners yet, so no one has to give anyone their cards, get anyone drinks, or light anyone's pipes.

Every hand after that

After the first hand all that changes, and the Bongmaster is always the dealer. At the beginning of each hand, the Bonghole gives their 2 best cards to the Bongmaster, and to repay the kindness the Bongmaster gives their 2 worst cards to the Bonghole. The Midi gives their best card to the Lightermaster, and the Lightermaster gives their worst card to the Midi. And the rich get richer!

But how do you become supreme Bongmaster at the end of the game?

This is whoever happens to be the Bongmaster whenever everyone decides to stop playing. Big whoop. It will probably happen when a seemingly terminal Bonghole finally becomes the Bongmaster. Such is the Bonghole's fate.

So when do I smoke!?

1. When a four or a two is played, everyone smokes. Wheeee!

2. If you win a round by being the last person to throw down a Trick or by throwing down a two, you smoke. Well done!

3. If you win a hand, you get two hits.

4. If you're the Bongmaster when the game ends, you're probably out of weed.

APPLES TO WHAT!?

People are bananas for Apples to Apples! And why not? It's an excellent party game that tries to jam random nonsense words into some kind of sense. Maybe you've even played the completely fucked-up edition, Cards Against Humanity, which tries to jam hilariously disturbing words into some kind of bastardized sort of sense. Either way, if you've played, you were probably partying on the side while the game went on, but now you put the party into the game, so to speak.

Object of the game

🍂 Collect the most cards.

🍂 Get the most stoned.

What you will need

🌿 Apples to Apples or Cards Against Humanity

🌿 4–10 players

🌿 *Note:* In Apples to Apples there are Red Apple cards and Green Apple cards. In Cards Against Humanity there are White cards (which are like the Red Apple cards) and Black cards (which are like the Green Apple cards). I'm going to call the Red Apple/White cards "Bud" cards and the Green Apple/Black cards "Spark" cards.

🌿 *Note part II:* Cards Against Humanity is pretty rad, and you can download the entire game for free from their site, cardsagainsthumanity.com. You then have to print and cut out all the cards, which is sort of a bitch if you're a lazy stoner, but still, it's excellent of them to make this an option.

MAKING AN APPLE BOWL

There are times in life when you have to make something to smoke from out of practically nothing. All you've got is weed, some glitter, a packet of hot sauce, and some string. If you're clever (read: desperate), you can make it work.

If you find yourself in one of those situations and you happen to also be in an orchard, you can make yourself a delicious bowl out of an apple. Here's how:

What you will need
An apple
A narrow digging tool like a pen

How to make the bowl
Dig a well out of the top of the apple. This is where the weed will go. Below the wide well, dig out a narrow tube that goes ¾ of the way down the apple.

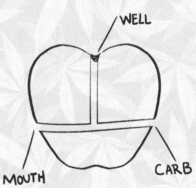

Jab a hole through the side of the apple that connects to the tube below the well.

Put the weed in the well, your mouth on the side hole, and smoke!

Bonuses

You can create a carb by jabbing a hole clear through the apple from one side to the other.

If you have tin foil, you can line the well with it to keep the weed drier. Just poke some tiny holes in the bottom so the smoke gets through.

How to play

1. Decide how many Spark cards need to be collected to win the game. The more players you have, the fewer cards this should be. For a game of 6 players, I recommend 6 cards.

2. Everyone decides on an alter ego they will use throughout the game. This could be your favorite *Arrested Development* character (Lucille 2, obv) or a historical figure, or a giant squid—whatever, it's your alter ego.

3. Everyone gets dealt 10 Bud cards, which they can look at but must keep secretly hidden from everyone else. The remaining Bud cards remain stacked face down.

4. The youngest player is the first to be the Picker, and they draw a Spark card and read it out loud. It'll say something like "Candy Bars" or "Lance Armstrong's Missing Testicle," depending on which version you're playing.

5. Everyone else puts down the Bud card they think the Picker's alter ego would choose. The Picker then decides which Bud card their alter ego would most likely pick. Whoever put down the Bud card the Picker picked gets the Spark card from the round and gloats like a jackass.

6. Everyone picks up enough Bud cards from the face-down pile so everyone has 10 cards again. Now it's the person to the left of the Picker's turn to be Picker. And thus the great world spins.

Special cards

Some Spark cards will have players lay down 2 Bud cards at a time. Just do that. It's not complicated.

Win!

You win when you collect the predetermined number of Spark cards it takes to win.

So when do I smoke!?

1. Every time you win a Spark card, you smoke.

2. If you win the game, you get a whole bowl-pack, bong-load, whatever, to your head.

2. *Consolation prize for the biggest loser:* If someone gets 0 or just one sad Spark card throughout the whole game, they get a consolation bowl-pack, bong-load, or whatever.

BEST BROWNIES EVVVVVAH!   Makes 12 brownies

Cannabutter

1 cup (2 sticks) butter   ½ ounce marijuana

Brownies

1 cup sugar   1 teaspoon vanilla extract

3/4 unsweetened cocoa powder   2 large eggs, cold

1/4 teaspoon Kosher salt   ½ cup all-purpose flour

½ cup (8 tablespoons) warm, melted cannabutter   handful or 2 of crushed walnuts (optional)

Cannabutter

Buds are best, obv, but you can totally use leaves if you have access to them. Since they are generally the throwaway part of the plant, you may be able to get them on the cheap. Or if you grow, hey, you've got something to do with your trimmings now! Stems, however, are off the table.

1. Finely grind up your herb. A food processor works well but a mortar and pestle is just as good. Gives your butter that handmade feel! A blender is best.

2. Melt the butter in a saucepan over low heat.

3. Add the herb and simmer on low heat for 50 minutes, stirring often. Breathe in the amazing smell.

4. Strain out the bud parts by pouring the mixture through a fine mesh sieve or cheesecloth. Really squish that shit with a spoon to get every last drop of butter out. Waste not, want not!

5. If you want your cannabutter in solid form, allow it to cool, then throw it in the fridge or freezer.

Brownies

1. Preheat the oven to 325°F and grease a 9x13-inch brownie pan.

2. In a heat-safe bowl, combine the sugar, cocoa powder, and salt.

3. Mix in the warm, melty, delicious cannabutter. Yum!

4. Stir in the vanilla extract and eggs. Mix that shit good.

5. Now gradually add the flour until everything is Sir Mixed-A-Lot. Add nuts if that's your jam.

6. Pour into a greased pan and bake that delicious fudgy goodness for 20 to 25 minutes, until you can stick it with a toothpick and have it come out clean.

7. Let cool on a rack if you can stand it!

Unboard Games

I'm sure you've got a shelf of games that you loved as a kid but are now just collecting dust since you discovered weed. Well, I've got good news for you and those games! With a little tweaking, you can combine them with your favorite adult activity for a night of smoky, stoney fun times.

And if your mom sold all your awesome games for 15¢ at a garage sale, Mr. Bud's got you. Visit www.ulyssespress.com /books/the-little-book-of-weed-games for a download of everything you need to play Battlespliffs (page 56), Cannabis Land (page 62), Bongs and Lighters (page 65), Cheeba Chess (page 71), and Draught Dodgers (page 74).

 # BATTLESPLIFFS

Hey, you sank my battlespliff, you a-hole! Or should I call you my hero? That depends on which version of the game you play.

Object of the game

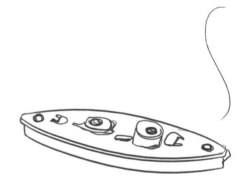

- Sink all your opponent's Battlespliffs.
- Smoke weed!

What you will need

- A tracing of the Battlespliff boards from our website (see page 55) or the original game with a similar name
- 5 Battlespliffs (guess where they are)
- 2 players
- Weed

How to play

1. Each player needs 1 Spliffs board and 1 Hit and Miss board. Set up your Battlespliffs, which look suspiciously like battleships, on your Spliffs board. If you lose your Battlespliffs, you can draw them on your traced gameboard. You need one Spliff that takes up 5 spaces, one that takes up 4, two that take up 3, and one that takes up 2. Got it?

2. The youngest player goes first. Player 1 calls out a position, like A-5, and Player 2 says if it's a hit or a miss.

3. Player 1 marks on their Hit and Miss board if it was a hit or a miss. Player 2 marks on their Spliffs board if one of their Battlespliffs was hit.

Score!

When a Battlespliff has all its coordinates hit, then kablooey! It's sunk!

So when do I smoke!?

Loser/Winner

1. You smoke every time one of your Battlespliffs gets sunk.

2. If you win the game, you get a whole bowl-pack, bong-load, or whatever, to your head.

Winner/Winner

1. You smoke every time you sink a Spliff.

2. If you win the game, you get a whole bowl-pack, bong-load, or whatever, to your head.

Power smokers

You can play either the Loser/Winner or the Winner/Winner version, but instead of every sunken Battlespliff equaling a hit, every hit equals a hit. A game takes only 10 to 20 minutes, so you'll each be smoking 17 hits in that time if you win/lose.

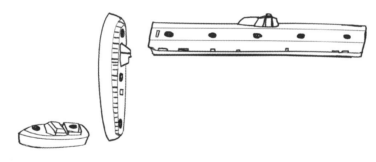

TWISTED TWISTER

You've loosened your mind with cannabis, so now it's time to loosen your body with some Twisted Twister. Get ready to twist and shout as you contort yourself in ways you never thought possible. Just don't forget to put the mat down first, otherwise you'll be hella confused.

Object of the game

🌿 Knock down the players who were once your friends.

🌿 Be the last player standing.

🌿 Smoke while contorted.

What you will need

🌿 Twister game

🌿 3-4 players

🌿 1 person to be the Spinner (don't worry, the games go fast so you won't have to be Spinner for long)

How to play

1. Play Twister. As you're making each move, keep an eye out for how you can move to screw over another player. Throw an elbow or a hip. Block someone from taking the easy spot. Generally be a dick. No two players' parts can occupy the same spot. Whoever gets there first gets it.

2. If there aren't enough spots for players' parts (say there are 4 players who all have a right hand on green and then the Spinner calls out, "Left foot green!"), race to see who can land their part on the spot first. Players who don't make it have to Mirror Swap whatever parts are down. (Say you didn't make your left foot to the green spot, and you already have your right foot on red, you have switch so your left foot is now on red. If you have multiple parts down, you have to switch all of them from right to left or left to right.)

Who won?

If you're the last one standing, congratulations! You're the most twisted!

So when do I smoke!?

OK, this is the interesting part, and how interesting it is depends on if you have the classic version or the new version that boasts a whole two new moves. Innovative!

Classic Twister game

1. When a green move is called out and all the players have moved, they must hold their position as the Spinner comes around with a bowl or joint and each player takes a hit. This will become more challenging as things get more twisted.

2. If you knock someone down, you get a hit. If you also fall though, the person you knocked over gets a hit. If you win, you get another hit!

New Twister game

1. Play by the classic rules, but if the Spinner lands on the cloud of smoke, everyone smokes. Hooray!

2. If the Spinner lands on T, indicating Spinner's choice, the Spinner gets a hit and calls out whatever move they damn well feel like.

CANNABIS LAND

I don't know how long it's been since you last looked at a Candy Land board, but that shit is insane! It is a psychedelic smorgasbord of munchie-tripped-out craziness where you travel a rainbow highway through an acid dream of staggering highs and perilous lows. Let us embrace the true spirit of the game with Cannabis Land!

Object of the game

- Beat your opponents to the candy promised land.

- Suffer from sensory overload by getting high and looking at the board.

What you will need

☙ Cannabis Land board from our website (see page 55)

☙ Token stoner character pieces also located on our website (see page 55)

☙ Cannabis cards from, you guessed it, our website (see page 55)

☙ 2–4 players

☙ Actual candy certainly wouldn't hurt

How to play

1. Pick your token stoner and line up at the start. The youngest player goes first by picking a cannabis card from the cannabis deck and moving their token stoner to the cannabis spot indicated on the cannabis card.

2. If you draw a card with a picture on it, move to the square on that board that shows that picture, even if it means going backward.

3. If you land exactly on a police-badge space, woe unto you! You lose your next turn as you wrestle your way out of a sticky mire of outdated laws and power-hungry cops.

4. If you land exactly on the bottom of a "pass," you race through the shortcut on the wings of an epic sugar rush. Wheeeeeee!

Crushing it!

You know you've won Cannabis Land when you get to the castle in the sky where all your favorite discontinued candies flow freely.

So when do I smoke!?

There are opportunities to smoke all over this board!

1. Every time you land on a heart square, take a hit.

2. If you get a double-heart card, take two hits.

3. If you land on a "pass," everyone passes around the weed.

4. If you land on a badge, when it comes time to skip your next turn, you take a hit so you feel less sad.

5. When you land on a picture square, that's right, take a hit, my friend!

6. When you win the game, you get a whole bowl-pack, bong-load, or whatever, to your head, if you can handle it!

BONGS AND LIGHTERS

While some board games from when you were a kid are actually kind of awesome when you bust them out again, some need major revisions because on closer inspection, they were actually kinda preachy. I'm talking to you, Chutes and Ladders! That's why I am giving you a whole new board filled with fun treats like bongs and lighters instead of guilt over eating cookies but rewards for baking a cake for yourself—just head on over to our website (see page 55)!

Object of the game

≋ Climb your way to the top of the drug game.

≋ Don't black out and fall down.

What you will need

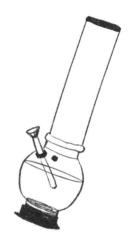

- The game board generously provided on our website (see page 55)

- Token stoner character pieces also provided on our website (see page 55)

- 1 die

- 2–6 players (aka Dope Dealers)

How to play

1. Line up at the starting line. The youngest player goes first by rolling the die and moving the number of squares rolled on said die. Then the next person goes, and the next, and so on.

2. If you land at the bottom of a bong, you get sucked up to a better square. Tubular!

3. If you land at the top of a flame, wah wah, ya burnt! You fall down to the bottom of the flame to where the lighter is.

4. If you land on the same square as another Dope Dealer, it's a Shootout over territory, using the die as a super scary gun. Highest roller shoots the

other Dope Dealer, sending them back 6 squares, which may actually be a windfall if the Dope Dealer who got shot lands at the bottom of a bong.

Kingpin!

You know you've annihilated the competition and become the drug kingpin when you're the first Dope Dealer to get to Dope Mansion in the tippy-top-left corner. The only way to get there is to land on it by exact count or travel up the grooviest bong of them all from the 79th square.

So when do I smoke!?

1. Obviously, every time you get sucked up a bong, you smoke.

2. Every time you win a Shootout, you smoke.

3. If you land on square 42, it's a social and everyone smokes.

4. If you win the game, you get a whole bowl-pack, bong-load, or whatever, to your head.

HUNGRY HUNGRY STONERS

Nom nom nom nom! If you've got an old (or new—no judgments!) Hungry Hungry Hippos game lying around, prepare yourself for a ravenous good time of hippo slapping, munchies devouring, and a surprising amount of cursing!

Object of the game

- Feed your hippo's face.
- Eat the most munchies.
- Smoke the most weed.

What you will need

- Hungry Hungry Hippos game
- 2–4 players
- Piece of paper to keep score on
- Spherical human treats (cheese balls, Gobstoppers, Whoppers, etc.)

How to play

1. Smack the shit out the hippo levers to collect the most hippo balls, of course! Once all the hippo balls have been devoured, count your hippo balls as fast as you can and shout out how many hippo balls you have in your hand. Then grab the equivalent amount of human spherical treats and eat them as fast as you can (you're the hippo—it's so meta!).

Score!

1. Whoever collects the most hippo balls gets 5 points.
2. Whoever finishes their spherical human treats first gets 5 points.
3. Whoever has the most points when no one could possibly eat any more spherical human treats wins!

So when do I smoke!?

1. For every 10 points you earn, you get a hit.

2. If you earn 15 points in one round, one of your hits goes to the saddest hippo player who hasn't gotten a hit in the longest amount of time.

3. Every time you take a hit, whether you earned it through points or by being pathetic, mark a * down on your score so you can keep track of who gets the next loser hit.

4. If you win the game, you get a whole bowl-pack, bong-load, joint, or whatever, to your head.

CHEEBA CHESS

They say chess is the game of kings. I say chess is the game of buds. Think about it. When you smoke you usually zone out really intently on something, be it a movie, a concert, whatevs—you get completely sucked into whatever you're doing. I contend that stoned chess will improve your game, or at the least make it more fun.

Object of the game

🍃 Capture the king!

🍃 Smoke all his weed.

What you will need

- Chess set, such as the one conveniently provided on our website (see page 55)
- Chess pieces, such as the ones generously given to you on our website (see page 55)
- 2 players

How to play

1. Follow the standard rules of chess. If you don't know how to play, this book certainly isn't the place for you to learn. I know this is a book on how to play games, but seriously, wanting to learn chess from *The Little Book of Weed Games* is like going to the dentist and asking him to look at your bum leg. Sure he's a doctor, but not that kind of doctor.

So when do I smoke!?

OK, now I'll tell you how to do stuff. There are two ways you can play this:

Weed makes you smarter

If weed helps you concentrate and get super tuned into what you're doing, this version is for you.

1. Every time you take a major piece (anything other than a pawn), take a hit.

2. If you capture your opponent's queen, take 2 hits.

   Optional power-smoker rule: Every time you put your opponent in check, take a hit.

3. If you win the game, you get a whole bowl-pack, bong-load, or whatever, to your head.

Weed makes you dumber

If weed makes you slower and a less logical, then instead of taking hits as rewards, you have to take them as penalties.

1. Every time a major piece (anything other than a pawn) gets taken from you, take a hit.

2. If your queen gets captured, take 2 hits.

   Optional power-smoker rule: Every time you get put in check, take a hit.

If you win the game, you deserve a reward! Plus the time for brain power is over. So take a whole bowl-pack, bong-load, or whatever, to your head. Woot!

DRAUGHT DODGERS

You probably know this game as checkers, but it was played in England long before it was in the U.S., and across the pond they call it "draughts." The modern version comes from an ancient game that dates back to bored Mesopotamians in 3000 BCE. Perhaps people were more easily entertained back then, because checkers can get pretty dull pretty quickly. But, as with most things, if you throw a little green at, things get more interesting in a hurry.

Object of the game

🍃 Take all your opponent's pieces.

🍃 Get high while doing so.

What you will need

≋ Checkers set, found on our website (see page 55)

≋ Checker pieces, located in the front of this book. Kidding! They're on our website (see page 55).

≋ 2 players

How to play

1. In case you don't remember, place all 12 of your pieces on the dark squares of the first 3 rows on your side of the board. Only dark squares can be played on in this game.

2. The player with the lighter color pieces goes first. Move your piece to an empty, adjacent diagonal square. If an adjacent diagonal square has an opponent's piece in it, and you can hop over it to an empty square immediately beyond said opponent's piece, then you capture the hell out of that piece.

3. You can zip around the board as many times as possible, capturing pieces in the same turn so long as you're moving forward, jumping over an opponent's piece, and landing in an empty square immediately beyond it.

4. If you worm your way all the way over to the last row of your opponent's side, then you get crowned supreme Draught Dodger! A piece of your color gets stacked on the piece that traversed the great divide, crowning you and making you awesome. This piece is now a Draught Dodger.
5. Draught Dodgers are allowed to move backward as well as forward. But other than that, they are just regular guys, putting their pants on one leg at a time just like everybody else.

Waiting out the war

As in regular checkers, if you manage to dodge all your opponent's efforts to capture you and enlist you into the war—hence the name Draught Dodger—and instead you capture all their pieces and bring them to your underground peace commune, then you win! But unlike regular checkers, you can sabotage your opponent and win the game samurai style if you are able to capture one of your opponent's Draught Dodgers.

So when do I smoke!?

As a Draught Dodger, smoking is part and parcel of your way of life.

1. Every time you capture a piece, bringing it over to your flower-power point of view, then you smoke. Hooray!

2. If you capture two or more pieces in one turn, you smoke for *every* piece captured.

3. If you get crowned a Draught Dodger, it's a social and everyone smokes.

4. If you win the game the regular way, you share a whole bowl-pack, bong-load, or whatever, with your opponent.

5. If you win the game samurai-sabotage style by capturing your opponent's Draught Dodger, then you win a whole bowl-pack, bong-load, or whatever, to your head.

BONG PONG

Everyone knows Flip Cup and Beer Pong are for beer lovers, but what about bud lovers? Well, Bong Pong takes everything you love about those two games, nixes the cheap beer, and adds in delicious ganja. And, yes, I know it's not technically a "board game," but you try to figure out what other chapter this game fits in better, smart guy!

Object of the game

- Get your balls in their cups.
- Smoke before they get their balls in your cups.

What you will need

- 2 teams that have an even number of players

≈ 1 packed smoking device or rolled joint or blunt for each team

≈ At least as many Ping-Pong balls as there are players (or throwable, spherical munchies such as malted milk balls, those big-ass Jaw Breakers, anything with some weight, though these will not bounce)

≈ 12 Solo cups

How to play

1. At opposite ends of a longish (about 8-foot) table, arrange the cups in pyramids of 3 cups in the back row, 2 in the middle row, 1 at the top. You may want to put some water (or beer, whatever) in the cups to weigh them down.

2. The team with the youngest player throws first. Toss or bounce the Ping-Pong ball and try to get it into a cup of the team across the way. If you fail, it's the other team's turn to toss.

3. Once a ball lands in the cup, your team must immediately take the ball out and rearrange the cups into the next pattern.

Cup formations

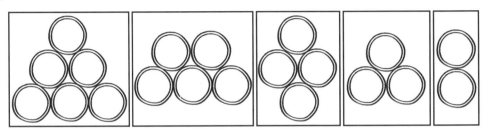

A champion is declared

. . . when your team has cleared all the opposite team's cups and completes the cipher for that toss. (See below for what I mean by "completes the cipher.")

Sudden Death Pong!

If, however, you land a ball in the other team's final cup but then they land a ball in your team's final cup before your team can complete a cipher, then it's SUDDEN DEATH PONG!

Each team lines up all 6 of their cups in one row at their respective ends of the table. All players launch their balls at the same time. Whichever team lands the most balls wins all the glory.

So when do I smoke!?

1. When you land a ball in the other team's cup, your team smokes in rapid succession trying to complete one full cipher (everyone on the team gets 1 hit) as your nemesis team feverishly takes turns trying to throw balls into your cups. If they get a ball in one of your cups before your team completes the cipher, then they begin smoking in rapid succession while your team rearranges your cups in the next pattern and then feverishly tries to land a ball in one of their cups. This goes on until one team completes a cipher before the other team lands a shot.

2. Whichever team wins the game also wins the remainder of both teams' bowls, joints, or whatever was being used to smoke in the game.

APPLE POT PIE   Makes 1 pie

Pot Pie Crust

2½ cups flour

1 teaspoon salt

3 teaspoons sugar

1 cup frozen cannabutter
(see page 52), cut into cubes

6 to 8 tablespoons ice water

Pot Pie Filling

8 Granny Smith apples, peeled, cored, and sliced

½ cup granulated sugar

¼ cup brown sugar

1 teaspoon ground cinnamon

Pot Pie Crust

1. Mix the flour, salt, and sugar together in a large bowl.

2. Add half the cannabutter and smoosh it together, or pulse it a few times in a food processor.

3. Add the other half and smoosh or pulse again until you have a course mixture with chunks the size of peas.

4. Add a couple tablespoons of ice water, sans ice, and smoosh or pulse. Keep adding and smoosh/pulsing until the dough starts clump up. It's ready when you can pinch any crumbly bit and it holds together. Don't overwork it, or you'll lose the flaky goodness.

5. Divide the mixture into two balls and smoosh them a bit.

6. Wrap them in plastic and throw 'em in the fridge.

Pot Pie Filling

If you cook your apples a little bit before baking them, then you can avoid getting a big, tall piecrust with a lot of air over a sad little layer of apples. If you don't care about that, just do step 1 and then move on to Getting Baked.

1. Put the peeled, cored, sliced apples in a large pot. Stir in the sugar and cinnamon.

2. Cook, covered, over very low heat for 15 to 20 minutes, stirring often.

3. Drain those apples through a strainer. Let 'em cool.

Getting Baked

1. Preheat the oven to 420°F.

2. Roll out one of your chilly dough balls so it's large enough to line your pie pan.

3. Line the pan, pour in the apples.

4. Roll out the other chilly dough ball so it's large enough to cover the apples.

5. Lay the dough over the apples and pinch the edges of the top and bottom crusts together.

6. Bake for 15 minutes, reduce temperature to 350°F, and bake for another 30 to 40 minutes, until the crust is golden and gorgeous.

7. Let cool on a wire rack for as long as you can stand without tearing into that mother.

Straight Up Dope!

What happens if you don't have any cards or board games? Maybe you're camping and didn't want to haul extra weight, or you're on vacation in a strange, wondrous country that's never had a patriarchal system leading to a deck of class-system cards? These games are made for just such occasions. They require no equipment or materials other than weed and something to smoke it with (OK, maybe a coin for a couple of them, but that hardly counts). Bon voyage!

HOLD IT!

Hold it right there! Put the bowl down nice and slow like. That's a good stoner. I stopped you from being a total fucking bore when you and your friends pass the dutchie on the left-hand side. I'll let you off with a warning this time, and a bit of advice: Next time you're smoking, try to Hold It!

Object of the game

☙ Keep it together.

What you will need

☙ 2 or more players

How to play

1. Pack a nice full bowl, blunt, etc. Take a slow hit, hold your breath, and count up to 15.

2. Meanwhile, your chums have that time to make you laugh and/or cough by making faces, telling jokes, or jumping around like the fools they are. Anything they can think of as long as they don't physically touch you (pulling the old sibling "I'm not touching yooooouuuu" move is totally acceptable). If you laugh and/or cough, you get skipped the next time the bowl goes around.

Score!

There's no hard and fast winner in this game. It's just a sort of fun, stoner-type staring contest meant to put some silly back in a cipher gone stale. It's also great if you don't have a whole lot of weed, because you know the old saying: You gotta cough to get off.

SMOKE AND BLOW

If you haven't personally played the party game Suck and Blow, you may have at least seen it in the classic '90s movie *Clueless*. Smoke and Blow is similar in that your mouth is going to get nice and close to other people's mouths, so be sure you are either really into the people you're playing with or at least really comfortable with them.

Object of the game

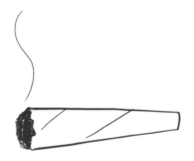

🔥 Blow smoke, and blow smoke.

What you will need

🔥 The more players, the merrier.

How to play

1. Stand in a circle. The youngest person smokes first. Take a nice, sizable hit, but not one that's so big that you cough. Turn to the player to your left, form a tunnel with your hands that connects your mouths, and blow the smoke into their mouth.

2. If they exhale smoke, you did it! It's still your turn, and you take another hit and try to blow it into the mouth of the next player in the circle. Keep going until you fail or you make it the full way around the circle.

3. If they do not exhale any smoke, you fail. Sound the sad trumpet. Now it's that player's turn to try to blow smoke into the next player (even if they are not the first player you blew smoke at, they just need to be the first person you failed with).

Score!

This game is about the glory and getting nice and close. It's best played when there is at least one person in the game you wouldn't mind making out with.

SLIP, SMOKE, OR STRIP

Here's another party game that you should play with people you wouldn't mind getting close with—or at least seeing butt-ass naked. Cuz that's about to happen.

Object of the game

- Get stoned.
- Don't get naked.

What you will need

- At least 3 players, but the more the merrier
- A coin

How to play

1. The youngest player flips the coin first and calls in the air what they think it will be, heads or butts. If you're right, you get a hit; well done! Now pass the coin along to the left so the next player can try their luck.

2. If you're wrong, take it off, baby! You must remove one piece of clothing. And if that piece is part of a pair (like shoes or socks), then you have to take off the pair. Don't be such a prude!

3. If you geek it and drop the coin, then you lose a piece of clothing and a little dignity because you have to do a little dance as you take off that piece.

Score!

Winning this game happens by process of elimination. Last person to still have a piece of clothing on wins! They get to finish off whatever smokable is being passed around.

 # NEVER HAVE I ALWAYS

It's time to learn some hilarious and totally embarrassing things about your friends! In this game of leading statements and begrudging confessions, you can find out anything you dare. A word of advice from Mr. Bud to you: Don't ask questions you don't want the answers to!

Object of the game

🍃 Get the juiciest secrets out of your friends.

What you will need

- At least 3 players, all with 10 fingers (OK, that's harsh; even the digitally challenged can play)
- Some good ideas in your brain

How to play

1. Everyone starts with 10 fingers raised. Or you can keep track using tick marks instead of fingers, since you're going to need fingers to smoke.

2. The youngest player makes the first statement, something like, "Never have I always sharted," or "Never have I always watched furries porn." It can be anything the player has never done. Or, and this is the kicker, only ever done once.

3. Anyone in the group who has done the totally embarrassing and weeeeird thing stated gets to smoke because they deserve a reward for letting their freakiness out or for having gone through something so fucking gross. They also lower 1 finger or put down 1 tick mark.

4. If you suspect the statement is something the stater has done once and you call the stater out on it correctly, then you both get a bonus smoke. High five! You do not get to lower a finger or make a tick mark for this hit.

5. If you suspect the statement is something the stater has done once and you call the stater out on it incorrectly, then you have to put up a previously downed finger or erase 1 of your tick marks.

6. Gameplay moves to the left, so after each statement, the person to the stater's left gets to make the next statement.

7. *Optional rule:* If the game is going slowly and no one has done the whacky shit the stater is saying, you can implement the rule that if no one smokes to a stater's statement, then the stater has to smoke.

Score!

You learned all sorts of strange things tonight. You probably just want to go home and take a shower. In a sense, everyone wins and loses equally in this game.

But the real winner is the person who gets down to 0 fingers or up to 10 tick marks. They are clearly the most outgoing—or unfortunate—member of the group, and they deserve to get a whole bowl-pack, bong-load, or whatever, to the head.

WELCOME TO THE THUMBDERDOME!

Get ready, ladies and gentlemen, for a bone-crunching, blood-spurting massacre of human flesh! It's going to be a horror show that will leave you as mangled shells of the people you once were! Or you'll just get a little giggly with none of that other stuff. Probably that actually.

Object of the game

☙ Obliterate your opponent's opposable digit.

What you will need

☙ 2 players, each with at least 1 thumb

How to play

1. Sit at a table and lock hands on top of it for support (and so you can't flail all over the place). Look into each other's eyes and chant in unison, "Two thumbs enter, one thumb leaves the THUMBDERDOME!"

2. Try to pin your opponent's thumb for 5 seconds with your thumb without unlocking your fingers or raising your hand off the table. While this is going on, each player smokes a joint with their non-wrestling hand and proceeds to blow the smoke in the face of the opponent, trying to blind and enrage them.

Score!

You must pin your opponent's thumb for 5 seconds using only your thumb and your killer instinct. If your hands raise off the table, the game is forfeited. If you unlock your fingers, get out of your chair—you lose, loser!

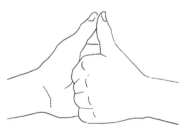

 # SAFE QUARTERS

This is Mr. Bud's personal favorite Straight Up Dope game in this book. It's simple yet challenging. It takes skill and dumb luck. You can go on a hot streak and lose it just as fast.

Object of the game

🌿 Hop your quarters into your opponent's holes.

What you will need

🌿 At least 2 players, but more is merrier

🌿 A quarter or similar token, like a Pog slammer (Remember those? Nah, probably not; you're too young!)

How to play

1. Sit around a table or on the floor in a circle so that everyone is an equal distance apart from side to side and across (i.e., you're not at a rectangular table). The youngest player tries to find Safe Quarters first.

2. Whoever isn't looking for Safe Quarters puts their hands flat on the table, with the tips of their index fingers touching each other and the tips of their thumbs touching, forming a triangle of empty space.

3. The player looking for Safe Quarters bounces the quarter, trying to get it to land in another player's triangle. The other players with triangle hands must remain still—they cannot move their hands to screw with someone's shot.

4. If you land in Safe Quarters you go again. If you miss, your turn is over and the player to your left gets a shot.

5. If you land 3 Safe Quarters in a row, you get to make up a rule. Something like no can say the word "lighter." If someone breaks the rule, their next turn gets skipped. If they are mid-turn, they immediately forfeit the rest of that turn.

So when do I smoke!?

1. If you land in Safe Quarters, i.e., someone's hand triangle, you smoke and you get to go again.

2. If you miss, your turn is over.

3. If your miss lands entirely on the player's hands but fails to fall into the Safe Quarter of their triangle, then they get to smoke.

4. If the quarter lands so it's touching the table inside the triangle, but still leaning on the player's hand, then you both smoke.

Score!

This whole game is a win. There's no one winner, because it's good times for everyone. You just play until you're done, which is probably going to happen when you run out of weed.

Let's Get Hiiiiigh Movie Games

Few things are better than getting really blazed to a cult classic where the beloved characters make you feel like a real winner with good decision-making skills. No matter how high you get, you'll never reach the heights of Thurgood Jenkins or the lows of Tommy Chong. But you can try! And these games will help.

Each one gives cues for when to smoke during each movie, and there are three levels of smoking to choose from. You might be a "Film Puff Buff" who takes all the smoke chances you can get, a "Mild Movie Goer" who wants to be able to stand up when the flick is over, or you might want "Just a Little Flick." Either way, your cinematic experience will surely be enhanced.

REEFER GOODNESS

Reefer Madness is the pinnacle propaganda movie from the '30s highlighting the absolutely ludicrous opinion squares had about marijuana (or "the dread marihuana" as the film calls it). It was at this time when friendly ol' weed went from a mostly harmless medical and recreational substance to a scourge that was sweeping the nation. According to the G-men, this cannabis menace caused once-upstanding citizens to hallucinate, turn violent, and go permanently insane. *Reefer Madness* has all that, plus some pretty jive dances. Let's watch!

Just a Little Flick

Pick just one of the cues below and smoke whenever it comes up.

Mild Movie Goer

If you want to remember a little bit of the movie after you see it, smoke when:

1. A newspaper flashes on the screen, spinning or otherwise.

2. A white dude looks totally terrifying.

3. Someone laughs maniacally.

4. A poor girl dies at a tragically young age.

Film Puff Bluff

If you want to get to $\frac{1}{10}$ the height of any of the overblown "marihuana abusers" in the movie, smoke when:

1. Some absolutely ridiculous claim is made about weed.

2. Someone says something misogynistic.

3. Someone is worried about "the kids" and what will ever become of them.

4. The kids are dancing their ever-loving asses off.

5. Jack does something pretty fucked up. You gotta use your own moral compass for this one!

 # UP IN SOOOO MUCH SMOKE

Cheech and Chong are two of the most beloved stoners in movie history. Oblivious, hilarious, musical virtuosos, they spend most of their time tooling around California (and a bit of Tijuana, naturally) in a blue shag—upholstered lowrider looking for some smoke (and some muff wouldn't hurt) as impressively idiotic cops try to score a big bust. Then they wear leotards. It is everything a stoner movie should be!

Just a Little Flick

Pick just one of the cues below and smoke whenever it comes up.

Mild Movie Goer

You're going to have to try pretty hard not to get too stoned during this movie. There are just too many golden opportunities! Take a hit (mostly) whenever:

1. You have no idea what someone said.

2. There is a nonsensical scene change and you have no idea how they got to where they are, but you're pretty sure the full story is now on the editing room floor.

3. Someone pulls a U-turn in the middle of the street or otherwise drives with incomprehensible recklessness.

Film Puff Bluff

This move is going to test your limits! You'd better put your seat belt on, man. I'll tell you that much. Smoke whenever:

1. Someone in the movie smokes. This alone is going to floor you.

2. Somebody goes to the bathroom.

3. There is gross overconsumption of narcotics that makes even you nervous.

4. Cheech sings.

5. Chong can't stand up under his own volition.

HALF BAKED-OFF

Can't you just see yourself ending up in the predicament of *Half Baked*? You and your totally harmless friends are just having a fine time when something random happens and you find yourself having to sell weed to keep your friend's virgin cornhole from being torn asunder. It's a classically relatable story.

Just a Little Flick

Pick just one of the cues below and smoke whenever it comes up.

Mild Movie Goer

If you're the one being sent out for tonight's munchies, you might want to keep the smoking a bit under control so you don't end up like poor, sweet Kenny.

Only smoke when:

1. There's a weed-induced hallucination, or any sort of hallucination really.

2. Dave Chapelle shows up as someone other than Thurgood.

3. Kenny cries.

Film Puff Bluff

I hope you're ready to hang with these guys, because you're going to smoke whenever:

1. They smoke.

2. Brian says "man" or Scarface says "B." Pick one or the other, not both, unless you want to run out of weed real quick.

3. Dave Chapelle as any character is holding a bunch of weed.

4. An awesome cameo happens. There are so many awesome cameos!

5. You think Mary Jane is being way too uptight.

HAROLD AND KUMAR GO TO HIGH CASTLE

The pot-fueled misadventures of Kumar and 'Roldie are stonertastic. Their quest for those perfect, juicy little burgers has it all: epic wins, terrible losses, hot babes, lessons learned, and a few well-earned tears. How better to come of age than fueled by a lust for fast food, the perfect woman, and justice?

Just a Little Flick

Pick just one of the cues below and smoke whenever it comes up.

Mild Movie Goer

Even Kenneth Park gets crunked in this movie, but if you want to be a pussy, smoke only when:

1. Harold acts the fool in front of Maria.

2. A CGI animal derails Harold and Kumar from getting to White Castle.

3. Harold or Kumar ask for directions to White Castle.

Film Puff Bluff

If Kumar's *sex* fantasy about the lady-sized bag of pot was eerily close to a dream you've had, then you should smoke whenever:

1. A white guy acts like a total asshole.

2. Something really, really fucking gross happens.

3. Harold and/or Kumar find themselves in the woods.

4. A skate punk says "Extreme!"

5. Kumar does something that drives Harold fucking bonkers.

Image Credits

Illustrations © Amanda Lanzone except the shutterstock artwork noted below:

Smoke throughout © Popov Nikolay

Pages 48 © Sergey Titov

Page 87 and folio leaf © Jared Shomo

Page 91 © Anna Rassadnikova

Page III man © Kamira; smoke © Popov Nikolay

About the Author

Mr. Bud has been a cannabis connoisseur for as long as he can remember, which granted, is not that long. He has traveled the world, mostly in his mind via the Discovery Channel. He is admired by college kids and disdained by his peers for discovering the one true fountain of youth: smoking enough pot to not mind living in your mom's basement.

About the Illustrator

Amanda Lanzone is an award-winning illustrator from New York. Her illustrations have appeared in the *New York Times*, *Popular Mechanics*, *The New Yorker*, *Adweek*, *Cosmopolitan*, and more. Lanzone earned her BFA at the School of Visual Arts, and she's received many honors and awards for her artwork. You can check out her work at AmandaLanzone.com.

Also from Ulysses Press

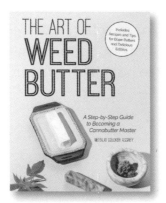

www.ulyssespress.com